GET A LIFE!

ELIZABETH I

W0090483

Books in the GET A LIFE! series

William the Conqueror
Elizabeth I
Julius Caesar
Florence Nightingale
Henry VIII
Queen Victoria
Marie Curie
Oliver Cromwell

GET A LIFE!
ELIZABETH I

PHILIP ARDAGH

Illustrated by Mike Philips

MACMILLAN CHILDREN'S BOOKS

*This one's for
the queue of our house:
Beany, the majestic moggy*

First published 1999
by Macmillan Children's Books
a division of Macmillan Publishers Ltd
25 Eccleston Place, London SW1W 9NF
Basingstoke and Oxford
www.macmillan.co.uk

Associated companies throughout the world

ISBN 0 330 37506 7

Text copyright © Philip Ardagh 1999
Illustrations copyright © Mike Philips 1999

The right of Philip Ardagh to be identified as the
author of this book has been asserted by him in accordance
with the Copyright, Designs and Patents Act 1988.

All rights reserved. No part of this publication may be
reproduced, stored in or introduced into a retrieval system, or
transmitted, in any form, or by any means (electronic, mechanical,
photocopying, recording or otherwise) without the prior written
permission of the publisher. Any person who does any unauthorized
act in relation to this publication may be liable to criminal prosecution
and civil claims for damages

1 3 5 7 9 8 6 4 2

A CIP catalogue record for this book is available from the British Library.

Printed by Mackays of Chatham plc, Chatham, Kent.

This book is sold subject to the condition that it shall not,
by way of trade or otherwise, be lent, re-sold, hired out,
or otherwise circulated without the publisher's prior consent
in any form of binding or cover other than that in
which it is published and without a similar condition including
this condition being imposed on the subsequent purchaser.

CONTENTS

The Author's Drastically Pruned
FAMILY TREE OF
ELIZABETH I
with some of the branches sawn off and a number of people missing altogether

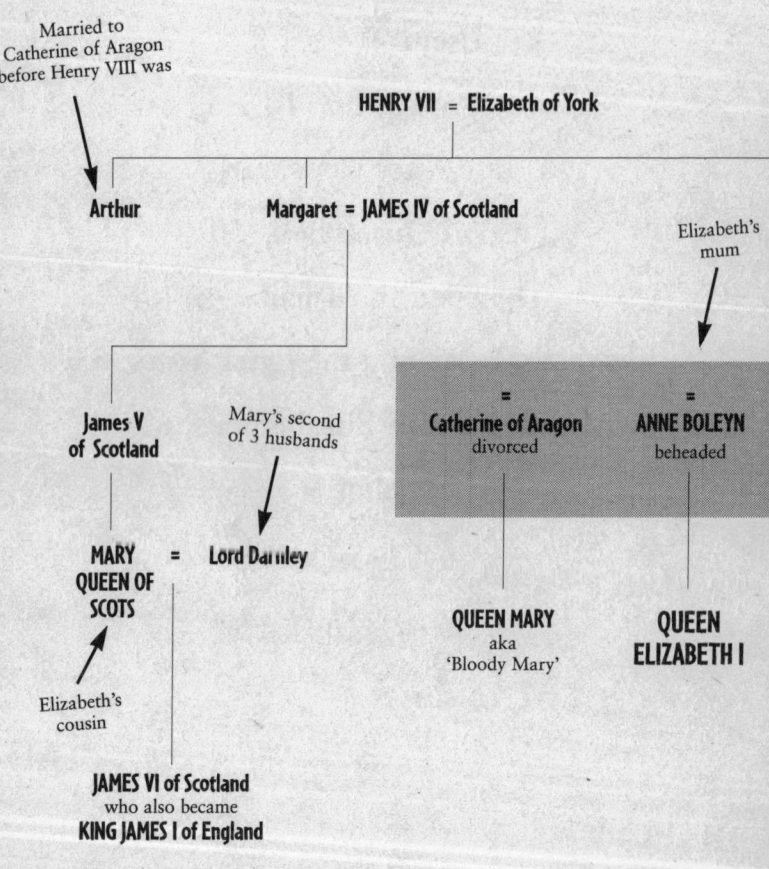

Married to
Catherine of Aragon
before Henry VIII was

HENRY VII = **Elizabeth of York**

Arthur   **Margaret** = **JAMES IV of Scotland**

Elizabeth's
mum

**James V
of Scotland**

Mary's second
of 3 husbands

=
Catherine of Aragon
divorced

=
ANNE BOLEYN
beheaded

**MARY
QUEEN OF
SCOTS**   =   **Lord Darnley**

Elizabeth's
cousin

QUEEN MARY
aka
'Bloody Mary'

**QUEEN
ELIZABETH I**

JAMES VI of Scotland
who also became
KING JAMES I of England

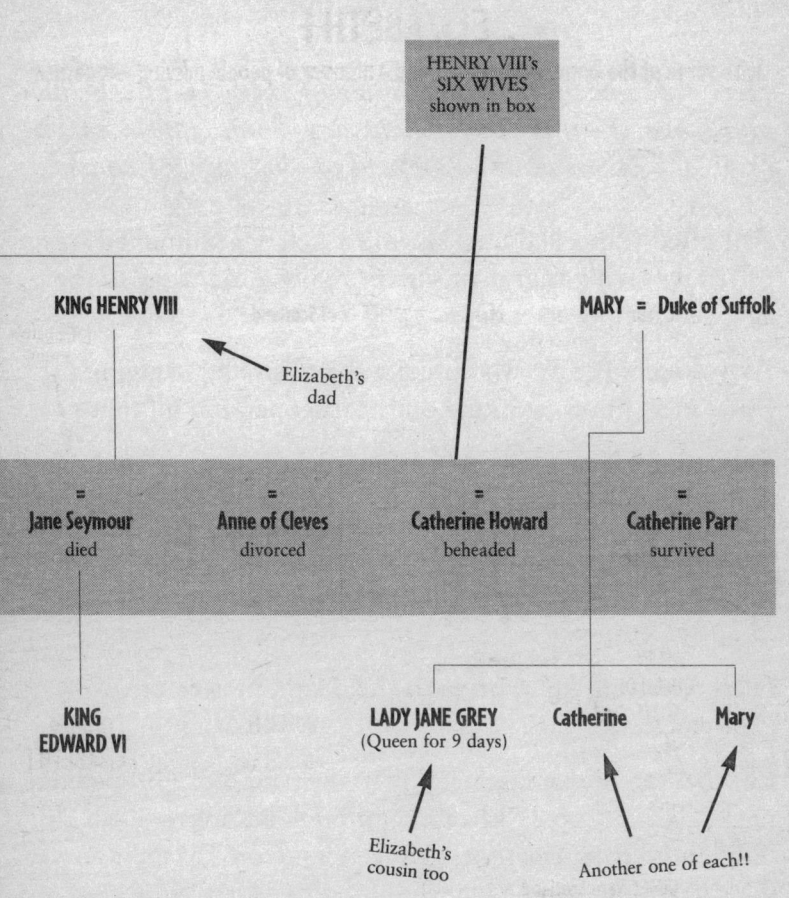

HENRY VIII's
SIX WIVES
shown in box

KING HENRY VIII

MARY = Duke of Suffolk

Elizabeth's
dad

=
Jane Seymour
died

=
Anne of Cleves
divorced

=
Catherine Howard
beheaded

=
Catherine Parr
survived

KING
EDWARD VI

LADY JANE GREY
(Queen for 9 days)

Catherine

Mary

Elizabeth's
cousin too

Another one of each!!

USEFUL WORDS
(Some more useful than others)

Here are some useful words. Some of them are Elizabethan and some are from the present day. Some appear in this book and others don't . . . except on this page, of course.

Annulled Cancelled out. Having a marriage annulled was officially saying that it was never really a marriage in the first place, honest!

Astrologers People who predict the future by studying the stars. (You know, working out horoscopes and all that.)

Beheaded Having your head chopped off. Should really be *de*headed, if you think about it.

Coffers Chests that money and valuables were kept in. 'England's coffers' is another name for England's treasury . . . often empty.

Duel A private fight, often to the death, between two gentlemen.

Elizabethan Something relating to the period of Elizabeth I's reign. (For example: 'Elizabethan England' means 'England during her time as queen' and 'an Elizabethan playwright' was someone who wroght – sorry, *wrote* – plays during her reign.)

Hedge-creepers Elizabethan robbers who pounced out on their victims from in or behind hedges.

Heresy An opinion that's different to the view of the official Church.

Illegitimate An illegitimate child was a child whose parents weren't married.

Prancer A horse. (A prigger of prancers was a horse thief.)

Regent A person who ruled on behalf of monarch if the monarch was out of the country, too young or too crazy.

Tudors Members of Elizabeth's family. Tudor was her family's last name, just like the Smith, Bloggs and Ardagh families' last names are Smith, Bloggs and Ardagh. (A Tudor house, for example, is a house built when one of the Tudor family was on the throne – from Henry VII in 1485 to Elizabeth's death in 1603.)

YOUNG LIZ

The pink, squidgy baby who was to grow up to be Queen Elizabeth I, one of Britain's most famous monarchs, was born on 7 September 1533. To be more precise, she was born in Greenwich Palace on the south bank of the River Thames. To be even more precise – and, hey, why not? – she was born in Anne Boleyn's bedroom, in Anne Boleyn's bed at around about three o'clock in the afternoon. In case you hadn't worked it out, Anne Boleyn was Elizabeth's mum. She was also King Henry VIII's second wife. (VIII is the Roman numerals for eight. V = 5 and III = 3). It would be nice to say that Anne was most famous for giving birth to such a fantabulous queen-to-be. But that just ain't so. Ms Boleyn is *faaaaar* more famous for having her head chopped off.

SSHH! SECRET SERVICE

Although, or perhaps *because*, Elizabeth's dad-to-be was King of England, Ireland and Wales, he and Anne Boleyn got married in secret on 25 January 1533. Very few people knew

about the wedding. It took place so early in the morning that it was still dark out! It wasn't until 12 April that year that Anne Boleyn appeared at her first official function as Queen.

RIGHT ROYAL MESS

One reason for the secrecy of the marriage was the mess caused by Henry divorcing his first wife, Catherine of Aragon (not to be confused with the herb tarragon). In those days, England was still a Catholic country and all religious matters came under the control of the Pope. Divorces weren't allowed, so Henry had argued with the Pope that his marriage to Aragon (the queen, not the herb) should be annulled. In other words, it should be officially declared that it hadn't been a proper marriage at all. The Pope wouldn't agree to this, which eventually led to Henry breaking England away from Catholicism.

LOSING HER HEAD

In those days, for some reason, many men wanted sons and not daughters. The trouble was that Henry VIII *really* wanted sons – or at least one measly son – who could grow up and become king after him. The reason Henry was so keen to have a son was so that the Tudor name could live on. Even if his daughter married, became queen and had children, the children would have their father's – and not the Tudor – name. When his first wife Catherine of Aragon produced a daughter, called Mary, he divorced her. So Henry then married Anne, and hoped for a baby boy . . .

... but, as you now know, Elizabeth was the result. This didn't bother Henry's subjects (and by that I don't mean Maths, French and Geography, but his people: the English). They lit bonfires in celebration and church bells were rung throughout the land, though mainly in churches, of course. Anne Boleyn, on the other hand, was probably more than a little disappointed that she hadn't been able to give Henry, her hubby, the boy so longed for, and was probably frightened too. (Talking of hands, Anne Boleyn had six fingers on one of hers!)

LET DOWN ON ALL SIDES

According to an ambassador's report, one reason why Henry was even more upset was that his 'physicians, astrologers, wizards and witches all ... affirmed it would be a boy' and a letter had even been written in advance that announced the birth of a prince. Now that had to be changed to 'princess'. The ambassador cheerfully went on to conclude that God had abandoned poor Henry!

THE NAME GAME

Elizabeth was christened in a silver font, underneath a canopy of crimson satin fringed with gold, on Wednesday 10 September. She was just three days old. The princess was wearing purple velvet with a long train edged with ermine (the same fur that edges lords' ceremonial robes). The end of the train was carried by Elizabeth's grandpa – Anne Boleyn's father – Thomas Boleyn, Earl of Wiltshire.

For some reason, the original choice of name was going to be 'Mary', the same as her older half-sister. Perhaps Henry thought all young girls looked the same so it would make life easier if his daughters had the same name? Fortunately, they settled for 'Elizabeth Tudor' instead.

OUT OF SIGHT

Henry didn't want a baby girl cluttering up the palaces, so he had little Liz sent to live in the country in the old wooden manor house of Hatfield. Anne had to stay put, though, so it was down to one of Elizabeth's aunts to care for her. Anne Boleyn stayed with the king because he wanted her to have another baby, but a *boy* this time. When Elizabeth was a year old Anne Boleyn did actually get pregnant again and with a boy. Sadly, he died before he was even born.

STEPMUM ONE, HERE SHE COMES

Henry VIII gave up on Elizabeth's mother after that. In his mind, she'd failed him and, charming chap that he was, he thought that it was all her fault. In the meantime, he'd found a new love-of-his life, a woman called Jane Seymour. But this didn't stop Henry from seeing his daughter Elizabeth. Delighted by the death of his first wife, Henry even had Elizabeth delivered to his palace at Hampton Court to take part in the 'celebrations'. He had Elizabeth brought into church to a proud blast of trumpets, and he later carried her around in his arms to show her off like a proud dad. Perhaps this was partly to show how important she was compared to Mary, his other daughter born of his disgraced, now dead, ex-wife.

GOING, GOING, GONE

Things didn't go so well for Elizabeth's mum. Henry started spreading rumours that poor old Anne Boleyn had been going out with other men when he wasn't looking. Because he was king and she was queen, this was a very serious matter. Anne was put on trial and found guilty of the charges. As a result, Henry could – and did – have their marriage annulled. Two days later, on 19 May 1536, she was beheaded at the Tower of London. (Beheaded is the polite term for having someone's head chopped off.) People often imagine that the executioner was some huge, burly bloke with a black hood over his head and a great big axe. In truth, the executioner was a very fine French swordsman . . . with a great big sword. So that's all right then.

THE LAST LAUGH

Sir William Kingston, Constable of the Tower of London, was surprised to find that, in the days leading up to her execution, Anne Boleyn seemed to be very cheerful most of the time. She laughed a lot and once joked with him that she'd heard the executioner was 'very good' and that she had a little neck. She then put her hands around her neck 'laughing heartily'. Perhaps it was nerves.

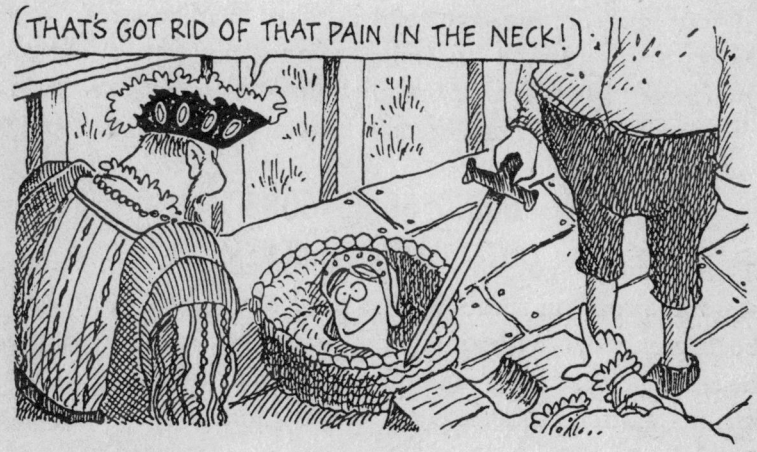

UNPAID BILLS

Although those who cared *for* Elizabeth were many miles from the palace, her mother still cared *about* her very much. Anne Boleyn visited Elizabeth often and, on her death, left a number of unpaid bills for expensive little items she'd ordered for her baby girl. These included caps made of taffeta and satin and even a crimson fringe to go around Elizabeth's cradle.

HEIRS AND FEARS

When Anne Boleyn died, Henry had three living children. His oldest child was, in fact, a boy. He was the Duke of Richmond. The trouble was, because Henry had never been married to the boy's mother – making the boy illegitimate – the Duke could never become king after him. Then came Catherine of Aragon's daughter, Mary. For a while, she'd been heir to the throne but, when Henry finally managed to divorce her mother, she was declared 'a bastard' and lost that right. Now we come to Elizabeth. With the other two out of the running, she then became 'heir apparent' (the next in line for the throne) . . . until her father had his marriage to *her* mother annulled just before her execution. When that happened, Elizabeth also lost her right to be queen.

OUTGROWN USEFULNESS

Now that Elizabeth was no longer such an important royal, things took a turn for the worse for her. With no more visits from her mother or father, Elizabeth soon grew out of her clothes without having any new ones to wear instead.

Things got so bad that Elizabeth's governess, Lady Bryan, had to write to King Henry's right-hand man, Thomas Cromwell, asking him to arrange for her to have some new clothes. This he did, as well as sorting out exactly how Elizabeth should be treated. Though no longer heir apparent, she was then officially recognized as the King's younger daughter and money was spent on her household.

BOUNCING BABY BROTHER

On 12 October 1537, Henry VIII's third wife, Jane Seymour, gave him what he'd always dreamt of: a legitimate male heir. If there had been bonfires and excitement when Elizabeth had been born, they were nothing compared to the celebrations that now spread throughout the kingdom. More than two thousand guns were fired from the Tower of London. Although only four years old, Elizabeth played an important official role at her half-brother's christening in the chapel at Hampton Court. She carried the christening mantle (or gown) but, because she was so little, she in turn was carried by Jane Seymour's brother Edward! Edward was also the name of the baby prince. Sadly, Jane Seymour died on 18 October, just six days after his birth.

STEPMUM NUMBER TWO

Elizabeth was six when her father married again. This, her second step-mother, was Anne of Cleves (not to be confused with cloves), a strict German Protestant. She and Henry just didn't really get along from the word go. So, by the following year, he'd managed to divorce her, throwing in two manor houses, their flashy contents, an annual allowance and the rather odd title of 'the King's beloved sister' . . . which everyone knew that she wasn't.

COUSIN CATHERINE

Next, Henry swiftly married the beautiful Catherine Howard. Catherine had been Elizabeth's mum's first cousin, which made her Elizabeth's cousin too! Because of this, she

showed a great deal of interest in little Liz and even gave her an important place at the wedding banquet. (The place you sat at an official banquet showed just how important you were, or weren't.) Sadly, Elizabeth's dad soon decided that Catherine, his 'rose without a thorn', wasn't quite the woman he'd imagined her to be. Like cousin Anne before her, Catherine Howard was beheaded at the Tower of London on 12 February 1542. Her headless body was buried next to the headless body of Elizabeth's mother. The poor eight-year-old must have been beginning to wonder what it was about her family that Henry disliked so much! She is said to have sworn then that she would never marry.

THE FINAL STEPMUM

Elizabeth's fourth and final stepmother was Catherine Parr, though her name was Lady Latimer when Henry met her because she had been married twice and outlived both her husbands. Catherine Parr was kind and caring to all three of her stepchildren. (The Duke of Richmond, the fourth – truly illegitimate – step-son had died before Prince Edward was born.) Edward loved her. Ten-year-old Elizabeth found her caring. Even the rather bitter 27-year-old Mary was delighted that the new queen recognized and accepted her 'royal blood'.

ROLE MODEL

Catherine Parr was an excellent role model for Elizabeth. As a woman she was well-educated, witty, clever and graceful. Queen

Catherine even stood in for King Henry as regent for a short time, while he was over on the continent leading the English army against the French. Unlike Elizabeth in later years, though, she had a king to bow down to. Elizabeth would go it alone.

ON THE WRITE TRACK

> I CAN READ THIS STANDING ON MY HEAD!

Elizabeth was educated at home. In the past, it hadn't been thought that it was worth teaching girls how to read and write, but that was before there were printed books. Then, in 1455, a German called Johann Gutenberg printed the first book and, more importantly in England, William Caxton set up a printing press over here in 1477. Now it was the done thing for all rich girls to be able to read them.

> WOULDN'T IT BE EASIER TO TURN THE BOOK THE RIGHT WAY UP, M'LADY?

LANGUAGE! LANGUAGE!

It was very important for royals to speak foreign languages – girls too – because, more often than not, they might be married off to foreign royals in marriages of convenience. (In other words, 'You can marry my daughter if you lend us a load of guns and ships to fight a common enemy.') Latin was important because it was the language used by scholars and the Church. (Not the building but the powerful Pope, archbishops and the like.) French was often considered the language of diplomacy. If you insulted someone in French it probably didn't sound as rude as if you said it in English.

As well as English, Latin and French, Princess Elizabeth could also speak Italian fluently. Her Greek and Spanish were said to be quite good, her Flemish (which non-French speakers in Flanders spoke) wasn't bad, and she knew more than a few words in Welsh.

BABY BRIDE?

Before the baby Elizabeth was even two years old, and still heir apparent to the throne, it was suggested that she should become engaged to the youngest son of the King of France, the Duke of Angoulême. One condition was that the 14-year-old Duke come over to England to be educated. Fortunately for Elizabeth in later life, the French king wanted the boy educated at home and, when the fuss blew up about Anne Boleyn's trial, he took her side instead of Henry's. The idea of the engagement was over.

HE LOOKS A BIT OLD FOR ME!

MISSED A BEAT

Elizabeth's education was quite unusual in that her tutor, Roger Ascham, didn't beat her. Beating kids was thought to be a very good way of teaching them things. Perhaps Mr Ascham didn't beat her because he thought it cruel. Perhaps he didn't do it in case her father got to hear about it and decided to chop *his* head off.

EXCELLENT REPORTS

By the time that Elizabeth was just six it was said that, even if she never bothered to have another lesson in her life, her knowledge would be a credit to the king. Roger Ascham went even further. He said that Elizabeth's mind 'had no womanly weakness, her perseverance is equal to that of a man.' If someone said that today, it would be taken as an insult, but back then in Tudor times, that was meant as a real compliment. Elizabeth was dead brainy and knowledgeable, and there was no argument about it. Aged eleven, she translated a whole book from the French, bound it in a cover she'd embroidered herself and gave it to Catherine Parr as a New Year's gift!

During Henry's last years, his son Edward lived with his daughter Elizabeth at Hatfield, and she and her half-brother and sister even had lessons together.

THE ROYAL LINE

In the Act of Succession of 1544, Mary and Elizabeth were officially placed in line to the throne after Edward and any of Henry's children which Catherine Parr might have. In other words they were far further down the pecking order than they had been before, but at least they were back on the list after having been struck off altogether. They were officially back in line to the throne, even if not first in line. They were princesses, not 'ladies', once more.

LIFE AFTER HENRY

Wlizabeth's father, Henry VIII, died in January 1547. Her stepbrother, crowned Edward VI, was only nine years old. The real power lay with the Lord Protector Edward Seymour (who had carried Elizabeth at Prince Edward's christening) and Cardinal Thomas Cranmer (who'd been Henry's right-hand man after Cromwell). They proved an unpopular combination and, after it was agreed that a peasants' revolt wasn't dealt with strongly enough, Seymour soon lost power and ended up being hanged.

ELIZABETH AND THE OTHER SEYMOUR

When Henry died, Elizabeth's stepmother, Catherine Parr (now widowed for the third time) married one of the Seymours — Edward's brother Thomas. Being married to the ex-Queen of England must have given Thomas Seymour big ambitions because, when she died, Seymour then turned his attention to Elizabeth. Soon rumours were flying about that they would marry next. It never happened. He was sent to the Tower of London along with two other members of Elizabeth's household, now back in Hatfield.

Then rumours started that Elizabeth was pregnant with his child. She knew the importance of public opinion — of what ordinary men and women felt — so asked to visit the new king, to show that she had nothing to hide. This was refused.

THE SICKLY KING

Edward had always been a sickly prince and, as king, he got no better. When he misbehaved or did badly in lessons – just because he was king now didn't mean his education ground to a halt – *he* wasn't the one to be beaten or whipped . . . it was someone else's job to stand in for him: the whipping boy's! Then Edward caught tuberculosis. He started coughing up blood. Soon he'd given up eating, was covered in sores, his hair was falling out and so were his fingernails and toenails. He died on 6 July 1553. Elizabeth had just moved up one place in line for the throne.

NO, NOT MARY YET

With Edward dead and Catherine Parr having had no children with Henry, you might expect that Mary was the next to be crowned. WRONG. Act of Succession or no Act of Succession, the Protestants who were now the real power behind the throne saw Mary as a dreaded C-A-T-H-O-L-I-C. (Remember, even Henry had been a fully-fledged Catholic before he broke away from the Pope and 'The Church of England' was born.) They chose the granddaughter of Henry's sister to be queen instead! Called Lady Jane Grey, she was forced into the role.

NINE DAY WONDER

'Queen Jane' was on the throne for exactly nine days – yes, you read that right the first time, nine *days* – before Mary's supporters swept Mary into power. You can probably guess what happened to Jane in 1554, even though she was only sixteen. Yup, off with her head.

BLOODY MARY

So now Elizabeth's older half-sister was on the throne at last. If she died, then Elizabeth could end up queen if she wasn't careful, so Mary thought it important to marry and have kids. The man she chose to marry had a brilliant name (Philip) but was a Catholic and King of Spain, which didn't make him a wildly popular choice with her subjects. Another thing which made Mary unpopular was that she was very strict about heresy. In her father's 38-year reign he had 81 people put to death for heresy. In Mary's five-year reign she had 280 put to death. That's an average of 56 people a year instead of Henry's 2.13 . . . though how you put 0.13 of a heretic to death without hurting the remaining 0.87 of him/her, is another matter! Anyway, you can see how she earned the nickname Bloody Mary.

ELIZABETH MEETS MARY

Mary (now Queen) and Elizabeth (now heir apparent) met at Aldgate and entered London with Elizabeth in place of honour behind the new queen. After which, Elizabeth spent much of her time in Mary's court . . . The trouble was that Elizabeth didn't want to be seen to be too strongly connected with unpopular Catholicism, and Mary, in turn, was suspicious of her much younger, and apparently more popular half-sister! In 1554 these matters were solved. Elizabeth was accused of plotting against Bloody Mary and was sent to the Tower!

PRISONER!

It must have been a frightening time for Elizabeth. Her mother had been beheaded at the Tower. Her cousin Catherine Howard had been beheaded at the Tower . . . and now here she was. She didn't get special treatment either – her cell was opposite the passageway leading to the loos. A few months later however, on 19 May 1554, Elizabeth was taken to Oxfordshire and the rather tatty palace of Woodstock. She was still a prisoner, but away from that dreadful place. Mary wanted to marry her off to some foreigner who would take her abroad and out of the way!

LOSING HOPE

Elizabeth's future looked far from sunny. To make her own right to be on the throne watertight, Mary had passed an act saying that her father's divorce from her mother Catherine of Aragon had been illegal. The knock-on effect of this was that it meant Henry's marriage to Elizabeth's mum, Anne Boleyn, was even more bogus and that Elizabeth was even more illegitimate (if such a thing were possible)! Then Mary appeared to get pregnant, and Elizabeth's chances of ever becoming queen looked very slim. As it turned out, Mary was only imagining things. She never had a child. In 1556, now back in Hatfield and amongst old friends, Elizabeth once again made it clear that she wouldn't marry, whatever anyone else might want.

BYE BYE, BLOODY MARY

Mary managed to make herself even more unpopular with her subjects (the English, Irish and Welsh, but not the Scots who had their own monarch). Over on the continent, her forces lost the town of Calais to the French, which had been under English control for 200 years. 'When I am dead and opened, you shall find Calais written on my heart,' she said, realizing the seriousness of the loss. She died of cancer on 17 November 1558. News soon reached the 25-year-old Elizabeth that, despite everything, she was now Queen of England!

GOOD QUEEN BESS

When Elizabeth became Queen of England, she wasn't known as Queen Elizabeth the First, because no one knew that there would be a Queen Elizabeth the Second coming to the throne in 1952. She was simply Queen Elizabeth. Later, she was given other nicknames, including 'Gloriana' and 'Good Queen Bess' . . . but not all to her face. It was safer to call her 'Your Gracious Majesty' or something equally grovelling.

PUBLIC DUTY

From the word go, Elizabeth knew how important it was to get the people on her side. When she rode into London on 14 January 1559, the day before her coronation, she made a point of waving and smiling at the huge crowds of people who had come out onto the streets to greet her – instead of looking stuck-up and haughty like many kings and queens had done before her.

PUBLIC FACE - THE MASK OF BEAUTY

Today, we'd describe Elizabeth as being brilliant at 'public relations'. In the days long before photographs, film and television, she found a way of controlling how people saw her. She created something called 'the mask of beauty'. It was a template – a strict pattern – which every single artist had to follow when drawing a picture or painting a portrait of her. In this way, she could be sure that she appeared the same in every portrait, so people would think that this was what she really looked like . . . and that look was 'beautiful'.

DEE TIME

Elizabeth chose to have her coronation on 15 January 1559 because that was the date recommended to her by the famous scientist Dr John Dee. He wasn't what we'd call a scientist today. For a start, he never wore a white lab coat but usually dressed in black. Not only that, he also dabbled in magic and astrology. His assistant Kelly claimed to see things in a crystal ball which he would tell Dr Dee about. Dee would then work out their meaning . . . and this is how he came up with the lucky date for the coronation.

CORONATION CAPERS

If this was a lucky date for the coronation, it's hard to imagine what it'd have been like on an *un*lucky one. The

crowds of well-wishers were so excited to be present at such an important and joyful occasion – Bloody Mary having been so unpopular with most of them – that they decided they wanted souvenirs to remember the day by. There was a beautiful blue (not red, don't believe everything you read) carpet which had been laid out for the Queen to walk from Westminster Hall to the Abbey. Someone had the smart idea of cutting out a tiny piece of carpet to keep. After all, who would notice such a small hole? No one. But once *loads* of people had cut out pieces, the holes became bigger, and there were lots of them! Elizabeth proved to be very good at dodging them but the poor old Duchess of Norfolk, who was holding the end of the Queen's train, kept on tripping and stumbling over them.

MARRIED TO HER COUNTRY

By now it was beginning to dawn on her courtiers that when she *said* she wasn't going to marry, she *meant* she wasn't going to marry. This was amazing for a number of reasons.

Firstly, because she was a woman and shouldn't women have a man to tell them what to do? (Don't punch me, I'm only explaining the feelings at the time!) Secondly, if she didn't marry she couldn't have any children to become her heirs to the crown. And surely she wanted heirs? Didn't *all* kings and queens want heirs? This was incredible! A free-thinking woman more interested in ruling for the here-and-now, than having kids for the later-on! Elizabeth explained that she was 'married to England', and gained a new nickname: The Virgin Queen.

MERRIE ENGLAND

After the harsh years of half-sister Mary's rule, England seemed a merry place under Elizabeth, although 'merry' was often spelled 'merrie' back then, but not always (because spelling didn't seem that important). Although still a part of Tudor Times, life during Elizabeth's reign later became known as the Elizabethan Age. It was the age of great writers such as William Shakespeare (I bet you've heard of him), Christopher Marlowe, Edmund Spencer, Philip Sidney and Ben Jonson. You can read about some famous Elizabethans on pages 62 and 63.

JUST AS SOON AS I'VE DECIDED HOW TO SPELL 'SHAKESPEARE', I CAN START WRITING SOME PLAYS!

ACT OF SUPREMACY

When Bloody Mary had been queen, she'd given control of the Church back to the Pope, as it had been before Henry VIII. Now that Elizabeth was in charge, she passed a law called the Act of Supremacy. This put the nation's Church under the control of the monarch (in other words, *her*), and royal officials, judges, clergymen and the like had to swear an oath of loyalty to her, or lose their jobs.

SCOTLAND OR GROTLAND?

Scotland's queen was Mary Stuart, the young wife of Francis, the heir to the throne of France. She was also Elizabeth's cousin. Mary Stuart lived in France with Francis, who later became king but, when he died in 1560, she returned to Scotland. Mary is said to have been very tall and beautiful while Scotland was thought by many non-Scots to be a real hellhole . . . and that's putting it politely. Mary Stuart didn't like the bad weather. She spoke French and most Scots didn't, and whilst she was a Catholic, most Scottish people were Puritans – extreme Protestants – but she was still their queen.

PURE PURITAN VIEWS

A Puritan organization in Scotland, called the Congregation, was very powerful. It encouraged a pure, simple approach to Christianity without what it saw as unnecessary trappings. Puritans were against statues and paintings in churches, and against rituals such as wearing wedding rings, and making the sign of the cross. They didn't want people wearing colourful clothes either, and dancing was certainly a no-no.

A WORRY TO ELIZABETH

Having cousin Mary up in Scotland was a worry to Elizabeth. Like Mary, most of Europe was Catholic, so against Elizabeth and England, while – just across the border – was this beautiful, young, Catholic queen.

Many people in Scotland wanted Elizabeth to marry the Earl of Arran and claim the crown of Scotland. A Protestant Queen of England as ruler of Scotland seemed, to many, a better choice than a French-speaking Catholic . . . but Elizabeth had no intention of marrying anyone. She refused the Earl's proposal twice, and the Scottish people felt they were being abandoned.

A CLAIM TO THE ENGLISH THRONE

As Elizabeth's cousin, Mary Queen of Scots wanted to be officially made 'heir presumptive' to the English throne. In other words, she would instantly be 'second in the kingdom' and become Queen of England when Elizabeth died, if

Elizabeth didn't marry and have kids. Elizabeth said that she was worried that if she agreed to this, Mary would become the centre of attention for plots to overthrow her and put Mary in her place. The good thing for Elizabeth was that, if Mary wanted to become Queen of England after her, she might have some influence over her cousin.

MR MARY

When it came to Mary Queen of Scots choosing a new husband, it was time for Elizabeth to use any influence she had. Mary was seen as a very good 'catch'. Already Queen of Scots and, possibly, to be Queen of England, plenty of important and powerful men wanted to be her husband. Elizabeth was particularly worried that if cousin Mary married someone from the royal families of Austria, Spain or France, she could end up with a power-hungry Catholic king right on her border.

Elizabeth decided to unleash her secret weapon on Mary: Lord Dudley. Lord Dudley was Elizabeth's favourite, dashing courtier and a bit of a smoothy too. Some historians believed that he and Elizabeth had even been in love with each other, for a while. Whether Dudley rejected Mary or Mary rejected Dudley we're not sure, but Elizabeth would have to come up with another match . . .

DEADLY DARNLEY

The man Mary did marry was another Lord, called Darnley. He was a real silver-tongued talker and good-looker and was despised by the Scottish lords. Once they'd got married, Mary found a new side to Lord Darnley – a nasty, rude side

which made her cry. He was a drunken brute, and Mary turned to her secretary, David Rizzio, for a shoulder to cry on. Darnley thought they were doing a lot more than that together so he arranged to have Rizzio stabbed fifty times right before Mary's eyes.

MORE MURDER

But Darnley himself came to an even more bizzare end. Ill and in bed in Edinburgh one day, he didn't live to see the dawn. On 19 February 1566, there was a huge explosion and his body went flying out of the bed, through the Edinburgh skies and landed with a squelch. Someone had blown up the house he was staying in! That won't have bothered Darnley, though. He'd been strangled before the gunpowder had even been set alight! Soon everyone knew that a man called Lord Boswell had arranged the dirty deed and, rumour had it, he'd done it for Mary.

MARRIAGE 3 – THE SEQUEL

No sooner was Darnley dead than Mary was forced into marrying Lord Boswell . . . but he fled the country when his enemies came after him. Mary was then locked up in a castle on an island in the middle of Lochleven (a loch or 'big lake').

INTO THE ARMS OF OUR LIZ

Mary managed to escape by boat, having disguised herself as a serving woman. (This sort of disguise crops up a number of times in Scottish history and it's not always a woman under that thick skirt and tatty shawl.) Powerless and friendless in Scotland, Mary now fled to England to 'throw herself on the mercy of the Queen'. This meant going to Elizabeth and saying something along the lines of,

'Look, sorry if we haven't always seen eye-to-eye, but will you be nice to me? I promise to be good.' She left behind her son James, who became King of Scotland.

STOP THOSE PLOTS!

Elizabeth let Mary stay in England – even if it was under guard and in the north, away from court – and, exactly as she'd predicted, many Catholics wanted to see her on the throne and took the opportunity to plot against Elizabeth. In 1583, Francis Throckmorton planned an invasion of England by Catholic Spain. He was caught, tortured and gave away the names of his co-conspirators. The invasion was over before it began.

An Italian banker called Roberto Ridolfi planned another invasion but his plot was uncovered by Elizabeth's secret service. Although Ridolfi himself was out of the country, so avoided arrest, the other plotters weren't so lucky.

OVER A BARREL

Of course, Mary herself could deny having anything to do with these plots. She could claim that they were nothing to do with her. She hadn't *asked* Throckmorton and Ridolfi to arrange these Catholic invasions. When it came to the Babington Plot, though, Elizabeth had her over a barrel. Babington wasn't planning an invasion, he simply wanted to assassinate Elizabeth and put Mary Stuart on the throne.

Elizabeth's secret service found out about the plot and Mary's own involvement when they discovered coded messages between Mary and the plotters, kept in water-proof leather pouches, hidden inside barrels.

GUILTY!

Elizabeth was shocked and dismayed when she heard the news. Not only had her cousin betrayed her but, if found guilty, Elizabeth would have to sign her death warrant. You couldn't have people guilty of plots to murder the Queen of England getting off scot-free. (*Scot*-free . . . Mary Queen of *Scots*. Geddit? Never mind.) Mary was tried at Fotheringay Castle in Northamptonshire and, indeed, found guilty. After much soul-searching, Elizabeth signed the death warrant but did not pass it on to her ministers. Finally, they decided that they had to take action on their own.

COUSIN MARY GETS THE CHOP

On 8 February 1587, Mary Stuart was executed in the great hall at Fotheringay Castle. The night before, she'd written letters to friends and given instructions as

PERHAPS THEY SHOULD HAVE CALLED **THIS** MARY 'BLOODY MARY'.

to who should have which pieces of her jewellery once she'd gone. Dressed in a black satin dress, it took two or three hacks of the axe to separate her head from her neck. Even then, the lips on her severed head are said to have moved for about a quarter of an hour, as if in silent prayer. Mary's head had rolled across the floor when the executioner picked it up by what he thought was her hair. It turned out to be a brown wig. Underneath it, Mary's real hair was grey . . . while underneath Mary's petticoat was her terrified tiny pet dog!

THE QUEEN'S FURY

Elizabeth was said to have been furious when she found out that her ministers had taken matters into their own hands. She openly grieved whilst the rest of the county rejoiced. Remembering what we said about Elizabeth being good at public relations, it is, of course, possible that she was putting on an act of sadness so that the Catholic countries wouldn't be so quick to blame and condemn her.

JIM LAD

Mary's son James, already King of Scotland, was so eager to become King of England when Elizabeth eventually died that he wanted to be on friendly terms with her. Suddenly, the situation between Scotland and England got a lot better.

THE SPANISH ARMADA

When Elizabeth came to the throne, England's coffers were almost empty, meaning that there was very little money in the royal purse. One advantage of England now being Protestant was that Protestants on the Continent, some persecuted by their Catholic rulers, came over to the country . . . bringing their skills and knowledge with them. These included everything from glass-making and silk-weaving to mining and metal-working. Soon England began to make more money in trade.

WOOLLY SUBJECTS

England's biggest seller abroad was wool, and that meant that the English and Welsh countryside was covered with sheep. Some people owned just one small flock but a rich nobleman might own as many as 17,000 animals. During the Elizabethan Age there were about three times as many

SSSHH! I DIDN'T HAVE TIME TO KNIT ONE

sheep as people! Elizabeth passed a law making people wear sheep's wool hats on Sundays. This meant more money for the wool traders, and more money from them in taxes to *her*!

RULE THE WAVES?

Being an island nation, England needed ships to trade goods. There was no shortage of intrepid sailors and explorers in Elizabeth's reign. Probably the two most famous of these are Sir Francis Drake and Sir Walter Raleigh.

THE GREAT SPUD SAGA

(Nearly) everyone knows the famous story of Sir Walter Raleigh introducing Queen Elizabeth, and England, to that now-familiar vegetable the potato, which she loved. The only problem with this story is that *he* didn't and *she* didn't.

Sir Walter didn't introduce the potato to Britain. Most people who worry about such things seem to think it was brought back by a mathematician called Thomas Harriot (not to be confused with the haricot bean).

It's said that Good Queen Bess didn't get to enjoy the potato because no one knew how to cook it. A group of nobles ate the leaves and stems (which are poisonous) and threw away the actual potato part . . . They ended up so ill that no one else in Britain bothered tackling a tatty for about another hundred years!

SIR WALTER RALEIGH

It was true, however, that Sir Walter was one of the queen's favourites. Pointy beards were all the rage (for men) and Sir Walter's was one of the pointiest. He also wore a large ruff – a big frilly collar, fashionable with men and women. As well having a pointy beard and big ruff, Sir Walter Raleigh (pronounced to rhyme with 'poorly' rather than 'pally.') tried to set up a colony in America, to make trade easier. He chose the place and called it Virginia after the *Virgin* Queen.

TO THE COLONY!

It was all very well choosing the spot, but Sir Walter wasn't the one who actually had to live there. He was too busy off doing other flashy things. Seven-ships'-worth of colonists set off for Virginia in 1585. By 1586, seven-ships'-worth of colonists were asking to come home. Life out there was tough.

Sir Walter tried setting up the colony again in 1587, but that also met with failure.

UP IN SMOKE

Potato or no potato, it was Sir Walter who made smoking tobacco the in-thing in England. You might have thought that smokers guessed it was bad for them because they coughed up black tar, but that was the very reason why they thought it was *good* for them! (It's a funny Olde Worlde, eh?) They assumed that everyone – smokers and non smokers alike – were filled with this evil stuff, and that smoking tobacco helped you cough it up. How wrong they were.

UNACCEPTABLE FAILURE

Later in life, Sir Walter led an English expedition to try to find the fabulous South American gold of the legendary El Dorado . . . He failed and when he returned to England, Elizabeth's successor (Cousin Mary Stuart Queen of Scots' son James) had him beheaded.

A HARD LIFE ON THE OCEAN WAVES

Life on the ocean waves could be as tough as old boots. There are actual reports of sailors cutting up their boots, boiling the leather and eating them . . . but that was only after they'd eaten all the spare candles and any rats unlucky enough to be caught. Rations were scarce and disease was very common. Far more sailors died from illness than in battle, with malaria and yellow fever spreading through ships like wild fire (which is like tame fire, only angrier).

The real killer, though, was scurvy (a lack of Vitamin C). If only they'd known that a diet of fresh fruit would have helped cure that.

ARISE, SIR PIRATE

About the only Elizabethan seafarer as famous as Sir Walter was Sir Francis Drake. Sir Francis Drake hadn't been born a 'Sir'. He was knighted for attacking passing Spanish ships and stealing masses and masses of gold from them . . . oh, and for sailing round the world between 1577 and 1580. He was knighted at a ceremony on board his ship the *Golden Hind*, during which Elizabeth's garter slid down her leg, much to the delight of a goggle-eyed French envoy. England was, of course, totally against piracy . . . unless it was the crews of official English ships who were the ones behaving like pirates. In this trip alone, Sir Francis Drake brought back about treasure worth about £600,000. That's still a lot of money today, but back then it was an absolute fortune and he gave by far the most of it to Elizabeth.

BOWLS!

Sir Francis Drake is famous for playing bowls. I don't mean he had shelves of bowls trophies, I mean that he was famous for being interrupted during a game of bowls to be told that the Spanish Armada was coming. An armada is nothing more than a fleet of ships, but the Spanish Armada is one of the most famous in history.

TROUBLE BREWS

In case you hadn't guessed already, England and Spain were sworn enemies. King Philip (good name) of Spain was the ruler of the largest and most successful Catholic empire in the world. Queen Elizabeth was the ruler of the now-prosperous Protestant England. She supported the Protestant Dutch in their war against Spain and her nippy little English ships were doing a good job of piracy in Spanish waters. Elizabeth and England had become more than a thorn in Philip's side.

THE ARMADA IS PLANNED

The plan was a straightforward one. A huge Spanish Armada of a great many *big* ships would zoom down the English Channel, destroying any English resistance. It would then reach the Netherlands, defeat the Protestant

Dutch rebels, join forces with the Spaniards already over there, then come back and invade England. It should all be over by teatime . . . That was the plan, anyway.

BIG GUNS

The Spanish Armada was made up of 130 ships with 30,000 men, 19,000 of whom were soldiers. They had 2,431 guns and 125,790 cannonballs to fire at the English and Dutch. The guns could only be fired with any accuracy at distances of less than 200 metres (especially when a ship was rolling in the waves). There had to be a break of five minutes before firing a gun again, or it could get red hot and even explode.

NICE ONE, CHARLIE

Like Sir Walter Raleigh and the potato, many people think that Sir Francis Drake led the English fleet against the Armada. Wrong again! That honour belongs to the English Lord High Admiral, Charles Howard. Despite the impressive seafaring title, he wasn't really a sailor. He divided the defending fleet into four squadrons – led by himself, Drake (now the Vice-Admiral), Martin Frobisher (who had sailed to some very cold parts of the world and even kidnapped an Inuit), and a man named John Hawkins.

HAPLESS HAWKINS

In 1567, Sir John Hawkins had set sail from Plymouth with six ships. His flagship was called the *Jesus of Lubeck* which may sound grand, but kept taking in water (which is sailor-speak for 'it leaked like crazy'). After helping out an African king along the coast of West Africa, Sir John and his crew then sailed on to South America. During a storm in the Caribbean, the *Jesus of Lubeck* started falling to pieces, which came as no surprise to anyone. What was amazing was that it had lasted that long! While waiting for repairs, the Spanish showed up, but Hawkins was friendly and let them into port next to his fleet . . . which was very foolish. That night, the Spanish attacked. They didn't like Protestant English ships trading in what the Spanish saw as their territory. Now the Armada was coming, here was Hawkins' chance for revenge.

WHY DO I GET THAT SINKING FEELING?

Jesus of Lubeck

READY AND ABLE

The attack was far from a surprise. Once again, Elizabeth's secret service was brilliant. English spies sent back full reports of Spanish preparations, whereas security was so tight in English ports that a stranger had little chance of getting near them. On 12 April 1587, Drake was given the job of making life as difficult as possible for the Spanish assembling their forces. He left Portsmouth and sailed into the port of Cadiz, destroying a large number of defenceless Spanish ships still being prepared for war! He even took control of six Spanish galleons and brought them back as prizes. As well as ships, he'd also destroyed stores and provisions and set back the Armada by at least a year!

ELIZABETH MEETS THE TROOPS

When the long-awaited attack came, it's important to remember that King Philip wasn't expecting a big sea battle. He intended to knock out England's 'inferior' fleet, then come back and invade the country with Spanish troops he planned to pick up from the Netherlands later. This plan was so well known that, as the Armada sailed up the English Channel in July 1588, Elizabeth sailed down the River Thames to meet up with the English army at Tilbury. She was dressed in white, from the white feather in her steel helmet to her shoes. Even her horse was white and she carried a silver baton. She must have been an amazing sight.

As it was, she didn't need to lead her army into battle. News reached her while she was still at Tilbury that the Spanish Armada had been defeated and what ships remained had fled into the North Sea!

SPEECH! SPEECH!

Elizabeth's speech at Tilbury is a very famous one. She told her troops: 'I know I have the body of a weak and feeble woman, but I have the heart and stomach of a king, and a king of England too!' If, by 'stomach' she meant the stomach for a fight, no one who knew her would argue with that. You can read on page 56 how she boxed the Earl of Essex around the ears, and she often punched, kicked or threw things at her secretaries. Come to think of it, that body of hers can't have been that 'feeble' now, can it?

ARMADA ATTACK!

Both the size of the English fleet and the size of its actual ships were smaller than the Spanish. What British ships lacked in number they made up for in manoeuvrability. They could move more quickly and turn around more easily in the cramped conditions of a ten-day fight in the English Channel. Yes, this was *ten days* of almost continuous fighting. The world had never seen anything like it. The English Lord High Admiral used many tricks, including sending six flaming ships into the wall of Spanish galleons, setting them ablaze. He also ordered his men to bombard the enemy with gunfire without any attempt to board the Spanish ships, which was unheard of. Why bother to risk men trying to climb aboard a ship when you could simply destroy it? Finally, the English were victorious!

DUTCH DELIGHT!

The Protestant Dutch were so delighted by England's defeat of the Spanish that they struck a special medal to mark the victory. Based on the famous words of the Roman Julius Caesar: 'I came, I saw, I conquered', they showed a picture of the Spanish Armada with the words: 'She came, she saw, she fled' written underneath!

LIMPING HOME

Defeated and downhearted, what was left of the Spanish Armada made its way home, sailing in a loop all the way up the east of England and then around Scotland and Ireland. Meeting with storms and disease, the Armada arrived back in Spain with half the ships it had set out with. Queen Elizabeth's fleet lost none.

ELIZABETH, ESSEX AND THE LATER YEARS

Although Elizabeth never married – and, at one time, even King Philip of Spain had been suggested as a possible husband – she certainly liked dashing men and had her obvious favourites. A number of times this caused a near scandal (which is like a scandal but not quite one). Take the earlier time when there were rumours that she and Lord Dudley were in love. Dudley's wife was found dead at the bottom of the stairs, leaving him free to marry the Queen if she asked him! There's no proof that Dudley had pushed her, perhaps she fell . . . but you can see why tongues started wagging. As it was, he ended up marrying a woman called Lettice (not to be confused with the vegetable – er – lettuce). Elizabeth gave the poor woman the charming nickname 'She-wolf'!

ENTER ESSEX

In later years, Elizabeth's favourite was Essex. If you think that sounds more like a place name than a man's name, you'd be right. His name was actually Robert Devereux. 'Essex' was part of his title, Earl of Essex, but people often call him 'Essex' for short. He became favourite when Lord Dudley died not long after the defeat of the Armada.

It's hardly surprising that the young man caught the Queen's eye. He is said to have been very tall for those days when, for some reason, the average person was a lot smaller than the average person today, striding about the place, leaning forward 'like the neck of a giraffe'! He also had thick, curly hair and sparkling black eyes. It wasn't long before Elizabeth had him at her side most of the time.

RIVALS!

Essex soon got jealous if he thought the Queen was showing the slightest interest in someone else. Once, the Queen watched another young man, called Sir Charles Blount, perform brilliantly in a joust. As a reward, she sent him a golden chess piece – the queen. When Essex heard this, he was furious and called Blount a fool . . . only to be challenged to a duel by him. As a result, Essex was wounded but, rather than feeling sorry for him, Elizabeth thought it was fitting that someone 'should take him down and teach him better manners'. But Essex was soon in trouble again, this time challenging Sir Walter Raleigh over some petty matter.

NEED AND GREED

Elizabeth obviously felt the need to be admired, and Essex was greedy for power, so the pair were good for each other. But Essex was reckless – he often did things without thinking and disliked authority. Once, he tried to join Drake on an expedition when the Queen had already told him he couldn't go! She called him back and gave him a right earful, but soon forgave him. Another time he handed out knighthoods to a group of his friends without asking Elizabeth's permission first!

A RAGE TOO FAR

However attracted she was by Essex's wit and charm, Elizabeth also recognized that he might, one day, play an important part in serving England. He was given a number of different posts including Master of the Horse and Master of the Ordnance . . . but he went too far. A new Lord Deputy needed to be appointed for Ireland and Essex recommended one of his enemies for the job. The reason why was obvious. The Lord Deputy of Ireland would have to live in Ireland so would be out of Essex's way!

When Elizabeth refused, Essex turned his back on her. This was a terrible insult to a monarch, so she hit him round the ears! Essex exploded in a fit of terrible rage and lost control. All male courtiers wore swords, and he grabbed his.

This was crazy! No one behaved like that towards their monarch and got away with it.

... BACK WITH BESS

Essex's enemies were delighted. At best, surely, Elizabeth would have him beheaded or banished? At worst, at least the Queen would no longer favour this headstrong young man who'd grown far too big for his boots. Wrong again. After a very short time of disgrace, Essex was back. In 1599 he was Elizabeth's army commander in Ireland – a position he loved because he'd always wanted to be a great soldier.

THE TROUBLED ISLE

Although Elizabeth was Queen of Ireland and Wales as well as England, Ireland was a particular worry to her for a particular reason. The Irish were Catholics . . . and there was a constant fear that the Spanish would help cause an uprising over there. It was thought that one way around this problem was to fill the country with Protestants, so colonies of Protestant English were 'planted' there.

CRUEL RULE

Not surprisingly, the Irish didn't like these people coming over from England and taking their land. Matters weren't helped by the fact that many English officials, such as the governor of Connaught, treated the Irish more like animals than people – and badly-treated animals at that. Soon, the Irish rebelled and, led by the Earl of Tyrone, defeated English troops at Yellow Ford in County Armagh. The

Spanish had planned to send a new Armada, this time to help the Irish, but bad weather forced them back. They didn't seem to have much luck with their armadas!

The English still had control of Dublin and the surrounding land, known as the Pale, and it was to Dublin that Essex brought his army.

DEFEAT AND DISEASE

Essex commanded an army of 1,300 on horseback and 16,000 foot soldiers, and leading them beyond the Pale, he confronted the Irish. Many of his troops were poorly trained, poorly equipped and had barely enough to eat. Soon, many fell ill. He failed to defeat the rebels or to win any glorious victories. This news didn't please Elizabeth back home so, in a last-ditch attempt to stay her favourite, he hurried back to England without even waiting for permission.

BEHIND THE MASK OF BEAUTY

Reaching Nonsuch Palace, without stopping to change his clothes after his long ride across country, Essex burst into Elizabeth's bedroom unannounced. He was still in his muddy boots. This must have been a terrible shock for the Queen.

What must have been a terrible shock for Essex was to see the Queen without wig, without piles of make-up, without her big ruff and sparkling jewels. Here was a balding, grey-haired 66-year-old human being! Amazingly, Elizabeth didn't explode with rage, though she had every right to. As well as invading her bedroom, Essex had also deserted his post in Ireland!

THE EX-EARL OF ESSEX

Again, Essex escaped with his life. Banished from the court, this time he openly turned against Elizabeth. It was *power* he wanted, not her. He sucked up to King James of Scotland and hatched a plot for an English rebellion. In February 1601, he and a few followers began marching on London, trying to whip up support along the way. But no one wanted to be in their gang, so the rebellion failed. Captured in his own home, Elizabeth finally had Essex beheaded on 25 February. His headless body was buried close to that of Elizabeth's mother, Anne Boleyn, which had lain there for almost 65 years.

SAD AND ALONE

As Elizabeth neared the end of her life, she must have been a strange sight. She stopped hiding her baldness under her bright red wigs, had no eyebrows, few teeth and her skin had been ruined by all those years of wearing dangerous lead-based make-up. But she did have the advantage of stunning (if rather strange) clothes, with over 3,000 dresses to choose from.

With Essex dead, she had no real favourite and was depressed and grumpy, convinced that people were plotting to kill her. She'd go about muttering to herself and stabbing curtains with a sword, just in case assassins were hiding behind them waiting to leap out at her!

THE FAMOUS FART

No book about Good Queen Bess would be complete with the famous fart story, and here is as good a place to put it as anywhere. Once, when a courtier was bowing to her before leaving her presence he broke wind. He was so embarrassed that he stayed away from court for seven long years. When he finally returned, he wondered if the Queen would recognize him, or how she would treat him. She took one look at him and laughed. 'Lord,' she said. 'I had forgot the fart!'

FAREWELL, VIRGIN QUEEN

In 1603, aged sixty-nine, the already weak Elizabeth got an ulcer in the throat and became seriously ill. She sat in her room for four days in almost complete silence, then was carried to her bed. Knowing that the Queen was dying, she had been asked who should have the throne of England after her. She is said to have replied: 'Who but my kinsman, the King of Scots?'

On 24 March, she died. The Elizabethan Age and Tudor Times were at an end. Sir Robert Carey rode to Holyrood Castle in Edinburgh to tell King James of Scotland that he was now King James of England too. England had lost its Virgin Queen.

OTHER FAMOUS ELIZABETHANS
(ALMOST IN ALPHABETICAL ORDER, BUT NOT QUITE.)

(c. is short for 'circa', meaning 'about/roughly')

Sir Francis BACON (1561–1626) Philosopher, writer and statesman. In 1785, it was suggested that all of so-called *Shakespeare*'s works were really written by Bacon!

William CECIL (1520–98) One of the most – if not *the* most – important men in the whole of England. Much liked by Elizabeth, he was her principal Secretary of State.

Robert CECIL (c.1563–1612) *William Cecil*'s seemingly serious son, who took over his dad's job when he retired. He appeared to be a dignified sort of chap, but loved gambling and parties, and his pet parrot too.

Sir Richard GRENVILLE (c.1541–91) Sir Walter Raleigh's cousin, famous for fighting against fifteen Spanish ships for fifteen hours with his one ship, the *Revenge*. Ordered his crew to blow up the Revenge rather than surrender . . . but they surrendered anyway. Sir Richard died of his wounds.

Ben JONSON (1572–1637) Soldier, poet, actor and – possibly – murderer. He got off on a technicality. Might have been a spy for the secret service. We don't know for sure. It's a secret.

Christopher MARLOWE (1564–93) A playwright who was also a member of the secret service. Supposedly stabbed to death in a pub brawl in Deptford. Some believe his death was faked for top secret reasons. (Sssh!) This is all very exciting, isn't it?

William SHAKESPEARE (1564–1616) The most famous writer in the whole world ever, *ever*, which can't be bad. He wrote poems but is probably most famous for his plays, originally performed at the Globe Theatre, London – watched by up to 3,000 people at a time!

Thomas TALLIS (c.1505–85) famous composer, mainly of church music. Was given the title of 'gentleman of the royal chapel'. Elizabeth loved music, but particularly dancing.

Sir Francis WALSINGHAM (c.1532–90) The head of Elizabeth's highly successful secret service, keeping her up to date with plots and plans at home and abroad.

TIMELINE
At home and abroad

1533	Elizabeth born.
	Inca Empire (of Peru) conquered by Spanish.
1534	*Turks capture Baghdad and Mesopotamia (now Iraq)*
1537	Edward VI born.
1546	*Michelangelo appointed architect of St. Peter's in Rome.*
1564	*William Shakespeare born in Stratford-upon-Avon.*
1580	*Italians introduce coffee drinking to Europe, from Turkey.*
1587	Mary Queen of Scots beheaded.
1588	Spanish Armada defeated.
1589	*William Lee invents machine for knitting stockings.*
1593	*Galileo invents a thermometer.*
1595	*Shakespeare finishes writing* Romeo and Juliet.
1596	*Tomatoes introduced to England.*
1601	Essex beheaded.
1603	Elizabeth I dies.